The Point ot Waking

*To Manou
love from Cora*

Cora Greenhill

Oversteps Books

First published in 2013 by   Oversteps Books Ltd
6 Halwell House
South Pool
Nr Kingsbridge
Devon
TQ7 2RX
UK

www.overstepsbooks.com

Printed in Great Britain by imprint digital, Devon

for Ian

Acknowledgements:

With thanks to the editors of the following periodicals, in which some of these poems were first published: The North, Tears in the Fence, The New Writer, The Interpreter's House, Staple, Artemispoetry, Other Poetry, Muse 7 (MMU), Bewilderbliss; and the e-magazines Antiphon and The Literary Bohemian. Some appeared in books: The Sheffield Anthology; and The Best of Manchester Poets 2 & 3; Genius Floored: A Shadow on the Wall; By Winter Hearths.

Unhinged was shortlisted for The Ver Prize 2012 and included in the anthology.
Unpainted Desert was shortlisted in the Friends of the Earth competition 2013, and was in the anthology Earthwords.
We Got the Hallstand was shortlisted in the Grey Hen Competition 2011 and The York Fest Competition 2013.
Ravenous was shortlisted in Holland Park Press Competition 2011.
Four Seasons: Notes was shortlisted in the Rhyme and Reason competition 2011 and appeared in the anthology Seasons.
Departure Lounge was shortlisted in the Bare Hands Competition 2013.
Several poems were in the collection Highly Commended in The New Writer's Poetry Prizes 2011.

Thanks to many terrific teachers, especially Peter and Ann Sansom, Mimi Khalvati, Sean O'Brien, Amanda Dalton. For encouragement and inspiration, to my friend and visionary poet, Rose Flint; and to Noel Williams for his generous feedback on the draft of this collection.

Contents

Unhinged

You're moulded in the hot hollow of your bed
like any creature not of the night.
But the creaks and crashes that wake you
aren't of the forest, and you're not holed
in the stable earth or safely nested
in the bole of a tree. You are asleep high
in the pink house near the edge of the cliff,
its flimsy fixtures straining for a fling
with this North Westerly, that has a trick
of unclasping shutters to slam against windows,
a knack of slapping awnings,
and shaking doors that ache to unhinge.

So, you must drag your sleep-sodden
limbs from their second skin, stumble
downstairs, wrench open resistant windows,
let the beast in, fanged and freezing.
You must fight to fend off its force
while you clamp the stiff catches closed
again, wrench and secure the latches
in their cold metal beds, burrow back
to the weak, wasted warmth of yours.
It's what you do. Wake up, slough off
the sleeping animal, work out
what in the world needs doing.

Four Seasons: Notes

Winter evenings sweat wet woodsmoke
and a bitter tar that drips from the zomba's chimney.
Ravens crunch the air like splitting kindling.
By midnight, sharp moonlight carries salt on its tongue,
stings with new snow from the mountains.
I hear *Death and the Maiden.*

Spring sweeps in with a hiss of swifts,
unzips its hoard of golds: sunspurge, crown daisies,
Jerusalem sage, in a *Hallelujah Chorus.*
And I'm listening for jasmine, but what I get
is orange blossom: notes flagrant as the cadences
of Toumani Diabaté's kora, or that aria from *Tosca.*

Summer is brittle, snapping pods and spitting pellets.
It's a raucous chorus of cicadas.
And the sexy armpit smell that slithers
through open car windows from the sticky weed
that stays green when the rest is straw.
This is Greece at fever pitch. Mastic oozes.
Scents are deep as carob honey,
dark as *Desert Blues.*

Autumn's first drops on hot earth release
the pheromones of hope, stir sea onions
to send out spires of light. But too early
and they spoil the grapes with mildew,
sour the wine. Half-dried sultanas rot.
Fermenting figs drop on the road,
stick to the ribs of our soles. We breathe
yeast, wait for a drenching.

Well of Sheep

At no point do they bleat.
I'm passing the well and just hear a rustle.
They must have reached too far
to get at those fig leaves.
Now they're ten feet down on bare stone.
I offer them what's to hand: rock lettuce,
pelleted stalks of late asphodels.
They sniff, cautious, nibble, then munch.
There's not much more around,
only thorns, rock roses, myrtle,
and I don't know if any of that's edible.
I keep throwing down fig leaves, until
the ewe's eyes at last look up, meet mine.
Leaving something to starve to death
goes against being human, I start to explain.
Then think of tourists feeding kittens,
before catching their planes.
But that train of thought's too long
to follow, when I don't know what I can do
about these asphodel-munching sheep,
trapped in this dry well.
I've raised their expectations now,
but I'm still a stranger here:
I listen to the acapella from the trees,
fail to recognise the songs.
Have I heard nightingales?
The nicotine-gouged faces in the cafenion
will only assault me with words and looks
that can't understand what I don't
understand. It's mid-day. May Day.
The scent of roasting sheep from tavernas
drifts up the valley to us, perched here
on the gorge edge. I'm ready for lunch.
Bet your sheep are too. Not my sheep -
I've only just met them! *You fed them.*
But I was just passing, and... what can I do?
There's no one around! *Exactly!*
You can't just leave them here.
You'll come back to the stink of corpses,
then, after years, wool and bones.

Today

The boot's full of bulging sacks, heavy as corpses.
Free firewood. After lugging them in, trundle off
down donkey mountain. A scatter of goat turds
on the road glows like dark chocolates.

Better than horse manure for potassium,
Giorgos told me, after I'd spread
Leo's stable muck around the orange trees
banking on getting a better crop next winter.

I flick them into a sack with a piece of the wood,
lose patience, lift them by hand. I forgot the trowel
I used yesterday to edge out crowded century plants.
Century plants flower in ten years, not a hundred,

Giorgos said. Either way I'll quite likely be dead.
'Someone will see them,' I say to the road ahead.

2

Hungry, I hit the coast at Kalives.
Smell out souvlaki joint, still open in winter.
Carry pita gyros to the beach – a hot weight
in the hand, reminiscent of something.

See a tumescent rainbow prod mule-dark cloud
from a steel horizon on slate-black sea.
I want my hair to be these glorious, grisly greys,
to shine darkly, as my feet sink in clay, like today.

I want my food to be this good
when I'm this hungry. I grow more beastly
as I get older. Hands, clumsy on keyboards now,
reach for real tools: machete, pick axe, trowel.

I lose my watch, forget my phone. Alone,
warming my bum at the stove, I'm home.

Change of Hearth

One finger unhooks the weightless bunches
from the hearth: rosemary, sage and bay,
dried away from the glare of summer.
With two hands, I remove a mask of Demeter,
smiling pensively behind her harvest.

Coal sack clouds have blacked out the mountains
for days. Time to retrieve the iron implements
from the cobwebs in the corner of the shed,
where dusty heaps of olive logs are snug
with scorpions, woodlice, curled-up centipedes.

A mound of kindling: dry pine
with cones attached, snappy fig sticks.
The logs waiting at the sides of the hearth,
ready to nudge in with the metal hook.
Now, the hiss and spit, crack and split,

then, like a rush of wings, the flames.
Life has burst indoors, like a cat
from a storm, already purring; or children
rowdy and red-faced from snow. Hestia laughs,
her wicked laugh, flaunts her gorgeous glow.

And already, she acts spoilt and demanding
always shifting position, wanting re-arranging.
I tend her helplessly. For tonight,
I won't take my eyes off her: we'll outstare
each other, new lovers, burning together.

Inviting Danger

Motionless on the white
wall by the blue
stove, frozen by light
and endless space

       evicted from your dark, snug
       under-bark bed in the woodpile
       among all the other bugs,
       you're probably just lost

but so poised in your lethal
engineering, aesthetic precision –
inflated curvature of claws, symmetrical,
and up-curled sting, dark spring ready

       to unsnap. Like snake, inspiring awe.
       Like snake. Inspiring. Awful, too,
       in perfect otherness. Yet I do
       know you, love you, take you in

close-up: snap! Then nudge you tenderly
to a shovel; but now you're fast with fear. I jump
back, don't quite panic, sweep you up again.
At arm's length, I tip you on the dump.

       But is it far enough away?
       Earlier we'd found babies under a stone
       in the garden: maybe we're inviting
       a colony by leaving them alone, unlike

the millipedes and woodlice and the snails.
We all have our prejudices, but I've read
of ancients who depicted a scorpion
under the sacred marriage bed.

Borders

It was easy to find
the herb garden. A young man, dark-skinned,
put down his hoe to show us round
beds of rose bergamot, cinnamon trees,
five varieties of sage, a bank of blue hyssop.
He picked us leaves that taste of chocolate,
sprigs of things to sniff – savouries, thymes and mints –
pointing out subtle differences
like someone born to it.

Did you grow up here?

No, he's from a place in Northern Pakistan,
famous for cricket. He's walked here,
he says. Had to. Eldest son.
No, not Afghanistan, he almost laughed,
too dangerous. Through Iran.
Arrived in Thessalonika. No work.
Athens. No work. Terrible, he says.
A friend brought him here.

So you're safe now?
In this lovely garden in Crete?

He shrugs, looks at the soil on his feet.
I live over there, waving vaguely
at mauve mountains.
I cannot live in village. Police.
No papers. Papers only by marry.

I pinch out a smile.

Tagetes are piled on the drying nets,
bloody as sunsets.
The thyme is on fire, seething
with bees.

Olive Harvest

We milk the twigs with our fingertips, use rakes
to comb the coarse tree pelts. Brooms swipe
the highest branches, rain berries onto waiting sheets.
The old trees breathe relief. Our stretched arms ache.

We trample rue, brush against rosemary,
release their pungent scents. Pausing to rest,
our oily hands, the low bow of the winter sun,
a palette of whites on the slopes of Lefka Ori,

connect us with a timeless ritual, not ours
by right of blood or birth or even steady labour.
We bought the trees, but pay again in sweat, to savour

this hour: as day pours its gold libation into the night,
we pour rivers of purple, green and black,
into sacks. The green oil will smell like grass.

Star

Hers is the real *graviera*
aged high in the Sfakian mountains.
Today, she rams her knife
through the blackened rind
of a wheel of cheese,
right through the pungent centre
to the wood. She sniffs loudly
as she slaps the wedge on paper.
Tears star the counter and till.
Raw eyes accuse oatmeal walls,
grainy shelves she built herself,
home-brewed vinegar – her life.

Maria's as honest as barley rusk.
Story spurts out – the Serbian man
who left her with their child,
for a better life abroad.
In the narrow village world
she's ostracised.
'Can you believe it?'
Odysseus, her little star,
starts school tomorrow.
He wants his Mummy and his Daddy there.
I think I will cry, too much.
I think ... they will hear me ... roar.

Abandoned

Seven Venetian wells, stone-hooded, stare up
at her with olive eyes unveiled, open to drowning.
Another seven, concrete-capped like bunkers,

crouch under branches of a great *platanos*, that wander
wide as a people's exodus, shedding skin like snakes
from roots as deep and trunk as wide as wells.

Past a litter of plastic flowers by the churchyard wall,
the hidden entrance of a donkey trail worn smooth
by hooves of laden mules. Thickets of thorns that snag

like spite. Then sun-scrubbed tiers above the gorge
where stately cypress waltz on marble floors.
Bells so faint they seem to live within the ear.

Year after year she climbs in winter sun to find
this *temenos* of stone: the clean-rimmed threshing circle,
fig tree's well, corbel-vaulted shepherds' hut,

with flowers-of-the-wind, blowing summer's colours
on a wind-mown lawn. Abandoned in the breeze,
anemones. Violet, magenta, indigo, cerise.

Restoration

We see him finger the faces of stones, brushing away
dry clay and mats of rooted green, day after day, till curves
re-surface through his hands, revealing where veiled women
stole down stairways under walls discreetly high, he says,
while men talked their world into coffee-dark nights,
and cats kept watch as now.

He's waiting for local bureaucrats to rubber-stamp
an operation to restore his sight. Learning to read
the memory of marl in donkey trails and threshing rings,
and all that made this elegance of Turkish houses stand
and wait to fall, empty as pomegranates hollowed
by redstarts in winter.

And while developers gain permits to raze and build
with reckless speed, the past seems to shift in its sleep:
a bare arm flung out there, the slope of a spine stirred,
responding, like a patient, to care. As if it's dreaming itself
into life again, coiled round these operations of modernity,
their careless certainty.

The Doves of Aspro

Some evenings you can see them
on the ledges of old houses
gilded like closed eyelids
praying westwards

before they rise as one
into a wide parabola
all their curved breasts
on fire.

Above the village church
the high *aloni*
the hidden donkey trails
and gold-tinged terrace walls

flashing like foil
in aerial meanders
against storm clouds
they seem to silence

the stuttering rock breaker
the rumble of rubble
dumped on new slag heaps
the drone of the digger.

Some evenings you can see them
on the ledges of old houses
gilded like closed eyelids
praying.

Christt is risen

Security lighting, screens of 'phones,
even a torch – it never really went dark
in the church. Not like the cave.

And the talking and shuffling
never quite stopped, and the priest
emerged quite visibly from behind the screen
and the candle of re-birth spluttered
and the mythical moment at midnight
was blasted away by the bangers outside
as the boys lit the bonfire to burn
Judas Iscariot, and we all crowded out
in the rain, holding our ears, opening
umbrellas, watching for puddles,
failing to cup our candle flames,
which quickly blew out, so

we lit them again from each others',
bending close to the glowing faces
of strangers and friends, eyes shining
in the luminous dark, exchanging
smiles, smiles for new light, now,
only now, and now clearly,
Xristos anesti!

Easter Monday

Morning air still
has the chill of spring
in its veins

but we wake bleary
from too much blood of God
in ours

still heavy
with Easter's
spit-roast sacrifices.

We drink the blood of two oranges,
breathe basil
and singed cypress wood.

Spun light pulses
wireless
between geranium and lavender.

Paired doves
make love with the same three notes
an interval apart.

The single yellow iris
cuts its quivering *chiaroscuro*
out of carob shade

waiting
for the baritone drone
of the bee

to sense an entrance,
lever the velvet sepal,
bumble in,

and leave,
perfunctory
in its purpose.

Nothing Sacred

The warning tape was scattered ragged in the wind.
Her machete rang on stone, then stuck in space.
She heard stuff hit water.
The language didn't sound like modern Greek.
Nor were the sounds quite like a modern *laute*.
A kingfisher skimmed by: they're territorial.
The cave contained five graves of female saints.
For heaven's sake, what now? she heard one sigh.

Myrtle Accepts Containers

Lone species.
Associated with Aphrodite,
who hid behind it when pursued by Zeus.
Used in bridal crowns, bouquets.
The oil was used as antidote to stings
of scorpions. Tannin for leather
was made from its bark and roots.
Myrtle accepts containers.

I bought the shrub for its coconut scented
leaves and tiny vanilla flowers
for the pot by the back door.

And then I remembered the tree
at Moni Paliani: higher than the church,
and the convent grown around it.
The cobwebs in the canopy are thick
as hide with dust. There is no space
in matted branches where birds,
snakes, hedgehogs, lizards, bats and rats
have built and left their nests.
It is suffocating in there, dry
as birdbones, snail shells, beetle
carapaces, vacated snake skins.

Burdens of prayers, both appeals
and gratitude, clutter its lower storeys:
crutches, corsets, frames.
And human hands and feet,
eyes and hearts, on cheap tin plaques.
And the icon, just wedged
in there among the debris. A lamp
burning perpetually beside Her.
Agia Myrtia. Holy Myrtle.

Persephone's Return

                              Did her feet
sink in these trembling meadows
shedding flakes of skin like petals
of cow parsley among this gloss
of stems? Did her rancid breath
stale the lemon blossom scent?

                              Would her eyes,
squinting at this much colour,
have searched for sepia shadows
to match their own? Perhaps
the slender gladioli stirred
occluded memory of her unforced limbs,
and the cistus rose brought crimson
shame to her sallow cheeks.

                              Were her moans
drowned in the whirr of bees?
Here among the quenching canopies
of walnut trees, would poppies, deep
enough for a girl to drown in, have filled
her with dread ... that her bones
would be dry among thorns, cracked
for the marrow by the lammergeier
when summer had clawed earth dry
again?

                              Or did she sleep
stretched in the scent of this chamomile quilt,
dreaming she heard the purr
of a turtle dove, and sipped the sweet
from the honeysuckle's tip?
And the open lobes of an orchid
drew moisture to her lips,
and the tongue of the dragon arum
rose in her rested thighs,
smeared with fresh red
of pomegranate flowers.

                              And when she woke
did irises revive in her
the endless hope of blue?

Karfi

The highest sanctuary of them all.   R. Castledon

The roads to Lasithi still have to be long
from any direction
as they weave and pleat through the high Psilitoris.

Nowadays, in coaches on new asphalt,
tourists make for the floodlit Diktaeon Cave,
above the rows of shops: blue pottery and lace.

There, they are told, the godling Zeus was fed
from Amaltheia's horn of milk, till he grew taller
than these peaks, more thunderous than this sky.

But the roughest of tracks goes further:
cars bounce and skid, suspension screeching,
up to the little plain of Nissimos

rimmed by the highest summits. We park
near the lonely chapel under a prickly oak
with only stately goats to appraise us.

The path winds round
a fleshless saddle of land, slung
from bare crags.

Sun filters through the clouds
to seam traces of ancient terraces:
a displaced people once scratched furrows

on this secret, hammocked plain.
As pilgrims, we honour their last
and highest sanctuary again.

Our minds unroll and hang
weightless imaginings
pinned by mere splinters of knowledge

and one stern Goddess,
arms uplifted in a timeless benediction
like these limestone horns of consecration

on the edge
raising white arms against blue:
air-carved or axe-hewn?

That First Morning

The house a high ship
on the big open of morning
I, on the bridge
caught in the main beam
dazzled like a rabbit.

Neo Horio prickles through mist
above the lilac valley.
Swifts etch graphic designs
on curves of crystal air,
swoop close, skimming
seedheads from weeds,
gold dust from rusty dock.

I *am* mist and swift,
at one with white dove
homing on a volley of sunlight
and the quizzical blackcap
on his mallow twig.

And I *am* those lines of pines
spiking the brightening
sides of the mountains –
a steadily rising cardiogram

for now is the hour of the cockerels
dogs will be barking
and I'm listening for your stirring
behind the white curtain,
suspended between breaths

– think Artemis undressed.

Summer is

not full here.
She is dry and rattles,
she is clawed.

She is burrs on my hem,
the thorn in my sandal,
the ant's sting on my thigh.

She has engineered
an infinite variety
of husks,

an armoury
of carriage designs:
hooked, toothed, and spiked.

There are gliders and spinners,
pods sticky and smooth ,
parachutes, catapults

and ingenious explosive devices.
Her colonising will
is absolute.

Only the birds' songs
are fluid
and they are merely collaborators.

I retreat indoors, rub balm
on my unprotected legs.

Marika appears in the garden,
her arms full of apricots.

Tourist Trade

You're not shown into kitchens any more
to peer through steam in iron pots
of bubbling artichokes and beans
rabbit stifado, wild greens.

You don't see Agi Rose complain
in mime of her rheumatic pain,
nor laugh with Sophie at jokes half-understood
as she lifts lids, grins 'Good!' or 'Very good!'

The food is viewed now in the modern way,
out front, in stainless steel displays.
The men translate and heap our plates
and we, full-mouthed, heap them with praise.

But after dinner, if you take the time
to walk the narrow path behind,
you'll see, in shadow, black-clad figures
watering the rows of tired *vlitas*.

Or get up while white alleyways
are pigeon-soft at break of day.
You'll catch the scent of early toil
as vegetables make love with oil.

Peaches

September. School is back.
I'm on the beach, biting the flesh
of a soft, sun-ripened peach.
A cicada tuts from a tamarisk tree.
I think of my grandma, who once,
on a Green Line bus in Hertfordshire,
after the war, when I was four,
announced her disapproval of peaches:
All skin and stone.
Nowt between worth the money.

Anna, beside me, sumptious as a peach,
sprawls sultana golden on a beachbed
borrowed from an old man
toothless and walnut skinned,
who watches her all day
from under his tamarisk tree.
Anna doesn't mind. Whatever
turns him on. She has a bed:
he, food for fantasy.
Both have their peaches, free.

Hibiscus

Four pink cones uncoil in tender morning light,
revealing crimson stamens spiked
with saffron pinheads, their perfect shadows
pencilled on vellum petals

that stretch back and back
under the day's hot breath, exposing
magenta hearts like lipstick stains
or blood bruises. Their blousy glory

gluts the afternoon, until by twilight
they float exhausted in jade cypress shade,
and five fat calyxes stand stiff with budswell
in their race to replace them.

Tomorrow, as I sweep them up
limp as used tissues, I'll touch the flimsy
skin in folds between my breasts,
sense the loss of stretch between my legs.

The Point of Waking

The slub and slap of the waves were only
a restless ally to my toss and turn
that clammy night, and dawn had a dull veneer.
Stubbornly aching back and blear
from broken sleep, still I stumbled to the water,
as I had resolved, to swim. On surfacing
I catch a flash, a splinter of sea, a glint
like glass in air. Then, alchemically distilling
his perky form from black pumice, bright fisher king
surveys his day – with me alighting in it.

A Sport of Water

I call out from the beach
We'll meet here again!

as you brace yourself
on the restless board

harness
yourself to the mast

lean
in the pillow of the wind

swivel   hover
and swerve away

                    skirting
the muddle of bathers

                  razoring
glass waves

to a violet haze
in the lee of Akrotiri

        now at gull speed
        your transparent sail

        only a slit in the horizon
        you've cut with a blade of light

tricks of the wind and sun
can lose you to me

but how my heart
                 kites
for you

now you've escaped
my gravity.

Siesta

We relax on our backs
rocked by the levelling swell,
merge with wavering layers of light
marbled in blues.

Nikos is wading among rocks,
lean and keen eyed,
prising black clusters of spikes
with his bare hands and a knife.

When his plastic bag is bulging
he joins us for a beer,
offering a salt succulence
of red and amber labia
to our bread, the delicate bowl
of shell wiped clean with a crust.

Then he's off at a call from his wife,
and we to our bed
under the cool gaze of the mountains
slippery and tender as urchins,
open as oysters, clean
as clams from wet sand

The cheeks of green almonds blush
rosy as sunset
as the sky turns mother of gold.

Departure Lounge

I'd tucked the last of our green figs
in a thermal mug in your hand luggage
with these fingers now linked

to your working hands
that fix things: locks on gates
the windsurf sail, the cistern.

They played on my skin this morning
teasing out tension
between my shoulder blades.

And your eyes that look
at all of me
and your tongue ...

that time when I wept
with self-loathing
it licked the salt from the wound.

The queue for the check-in is long.
You tell me to go but I stay.
It's hard to find conversation.

When you reach the corner of the stairs
I text, *I missed you first.*

Flight Times

Swallows looped the jagged spine of Vrissinas
sharpening their shrill cries.
We lay, languid after our climb,
in a curve of crystalline limestone,
cushioned in chamomile, pimpernel and vetch.
Clefts in these rocks once held gifts for a Goddess.

Sucked to a crescent, this moon stings
the empty mouth of tonight like a strong mint.
The ringtone splattered sleep.
One word: *Arrived.*
You're there. Crash landed in my here.
I try to dream you closer: limbs, belly hair.

Till daylight makes the same arrangement
roselit in the window frame,
that it did yesterday:
the ice-cut mountains that still chill
the river and the bay. Yet you'd skim
out there every day, a solitary sail.

And now you're carting your case, heavy
with gifts of the Goddess: honey and oil,
along our lane, over the rush of bogwater
from Burbage, as it spills and purls
into the Derwent. *Welcome to our other valley,*
I text. *The swallows will follow soon.*

Bud

She's clearing around the *magnolia stellata*
they planted in memory of their unborn child.

Under the flight of white petals,
among docks, a single peony bud
wetly crimson, like clotted blood.

Fostered

Sockless, in wellingtons, permanent black
scum between toes, nails that clawed grit:
they were fostered boys for the farm,
fed like dogs with porridge, potatoes,
slab of white bread, smear of jam.

I could pass as poor, had tears enough
in my clothes, I thought. But no.
They led me through briars and rushes
to guiness-dark ponds gobbed
with frogspawn, filled my boots with it.

They stole eggs to boil on our Easter fires,
said it was allowed. But dogs
had hot coals put in their mouths for that.
We stayed out all day in a hollow of bracken,
I had to eat eleven.

They knew where wild strawberries
grew in among briars. Out picking,
they slapped up my hand
so my wee heap of red berries
flew everywhere. Deliberately.

Burbage Edge in Snow

The Ringinglow Road under its ice quilt
was terrified we'd slide, stick, and stop,
as I, with nothing to cling to, felt sick
at the skid I could see coming, cursing
you and my own stupidity, sure
we'd be stranded as the slow-flowing
stream of cars log-jammed. But we pressed on
to the top – we couldn't have turned anyway.

Testing soles and sticks for grip,
we trod on the rime-edged path
slung nervously, slush-slippery
above the glacial valley and below
the ridge's stencilled architecture
cut from cobalt blue.

Redvested climbers cling to the cliffs
like ladybirds crawling to the light.
Stretched on our right, Carl Wark's tan flanks
white-flecked, like brindled bulls,
whose quiet breath makes clouds
diaphanous as frost flowers on glass.

In the glare, we squint at walkers slithering
towards us, greet each other blind
as we sidestep centre to edge to keep our footing.

                       And the child

is fearless, trouser-sledging
that slab of granite, to land
with flaming limbs and fiery hair
in her family's warm applause.

As if we've punched through a snowdrift
between us, we crunch ideas for that thesis
you should have written years ago, but still could.
Resistance splinters on projects long kept on ice,
igniting the fuse of possibilities, like travel
that won't cost the earth, but will take us out
from under our plumped-up common sense
along paths we can trust to lead us

                                to our edges.

Desert Trade

Even the sky
is dust. Walls and streets
bleached mud: all shades of beige.

He seats himself before us,
a pool of blues, unwinds
a river of indigo from his face.
The dark skin shines like oil,
purple with dye that's bled.

Long, tapered fingers flash
their rings as he unpacks
treasure from crumpled calico:
amber, hammered silver,
polished camel teeth.

The bargain made, we pay.
He stays. Expectant.
The ceremony of trade
is incomplete. I grope
around for gifts. Find soap,
in hotel wrappers.

His sneer
reveals gold teeth.
A gleaming finger pokes
my flesh, its shades of beige,
as if its pigment
had been lost by washing.

Breathdance

to Francis Bebey

He breathes his songs through a short reed pipe.
There is no knowing
What is his voice, and what the sound of the pipe.

We don't have a word for music
in our language.
Music is the same as life.
We don't speak of playing the mbira,
(stroking the silver keys as voices fill the air)
We touch its sounds.
Now, I like you to sing with me.
'Na tonde wa'. It means 'I love you'.
We sing it to our children.
No, not like that. We sing it with a smile.

He does not smile, he is smiled,
and the light shines from us all.

I am drawn to a space on the ground
danced by the songs
and the big moving airs of morning.

African Soul Rebels

Baaba. Griot.
Between prince and supplicant,
shaman and sheik, you draw us,
souls first, to our feet,
enraptured in song
and the djembe beat.

On all sides they block us from the aisles:
arms folded, thickset, dark suits, shaved heads.

Open arms reach down to us, inviting,

but the stage is too high.

Between Ariel and Caliban, angel and abiku,
did he come from behind us, between
or beyond us? He leaps
to the stage, dreadlocks flying,
guards and gravity defying -
a spirit with feet in the djembe beat.

Four wrestle him to the floor.
They said, *The rules are very strict*
no one gets on the stage.
They said, *He might have been dangerous*
we have to protect the artists.
He might have been armed
he might have meant them harm.
We understand how it must have looked
but you must understand, they said
he rushed
he pushed through the crowd.
You must understand how it looked,
they said.
They said, *It's our job – we had to stop him.*

I said,
We've done this throughout history:
tried to stop the dancing
clashed with cultures
erased rhythms
expelled ecstasy.
I said, *This is racism.*
I said, *Can't you read energy?*
I said, *Have you never seen anyone in a rush*
of love?
A dance forced
by joy?
I said, *You can't police*
the spirit.
I said, *This is sin:*
to interfere
with what you don't understand.

I didn't say any of that, only pointed out
we'd all been invited up onstage –
and would you have treated me like that?

Surgery

Resin hurt the air with its antiseptic sting.
He'd shaved the feathered green from the branches
neat as a butcher slivering ham from the bone
then jointed the trunk of the ancient conifer
grown so close to the house it stole our light.

Now we can see the rowan from the stairs,
the sky over Frogatt, and the ghost of the horse
that grazed in Heather's field. And that's Heather
in her scarf! The operation had been a success,
they said: secondaries could be removed in Spring.

Tomorrow we'll wake to an astringent clarity,
snow laid soft as lint on swellings
of green mulch, the stump draped
in a pristine shroud, stacked logs
wrapped tight as mummies.

A Dream of Dying

smell of honey-mushroom heather
it must be plump summer

alone   with a skylark or two
their cordless voices
higher   further out
than she's ever been
the calling
is the last   to go
then it rings off

the stones shift in their circle

                    making space

but no one would notice

Your love of Wild Horses

You were steadfast in your passions:
Patrick Moore on the universe,
Van Gogh, the sea,
wild horses of the Carmargue.
All best seen on the small screen
in your firm estimation.
And Monet and Turner on postcards.

Your tangible universe downsized to your flat,
then your room, then your rocking chair,
which frustrated the hell
out of all of your common-sense family:
You need to exercise! Use it or lose it! we'd bark.

But you loved to watch the clouds
blown across the sky through your velux
as your mind travelled well-worn paths
to the void, black holes, the beyond, the big questions.

You'd shrunk so small by then
you slipped the halter of your life with ease
and fled the stable of your cherished home
on a wisp of breath

above your bed
a horse with wings: Pegasus
on a postcard.

Released

Night scent of late jasmine:
the flower Greeks gave
to departing guests
blown kisses
reaching only air.

And I see you still
in that seagreen quilt,
shrunken like these almonds,
blackened on the tree in winter.

A white silence
of owlglide
full
of its own perfection
drops
all of it
flight-feathers flared
talons down-stretched
onto the top branch
of the pomegranate tree.

Closing her cape around her shoulders
she settles to watch me, a stranger
cloaked in her losses.
A spindle of silence whorls me.

As if this weren't enough,
her lift-off swoops so near me
I am caught in the updraft
vacuumed, undressed,
sucked clean enough to see
you, my mother, who hunted
like an owl
pouncing on revelation

         fly off

your freedom in your claws.

Ravenous

It comes to me half-way through
our scrambled eggs and mushrooms
at home on Sunday morning – Sunday,
the worst day in hospital: a skeleton force
of agency staff and no diversions.
Ann has 'flu. I'm ravenous for rest.
I only know, finishing the toast,
it's what I have to do. Drive all the way
back to you. Four hours on motorways,
then Green Lanes: wet, clotted traffic.
I will find you propped up and protesting,
the nurses accusing. I'll feed you mince
and potatoes, yogurt and tinned fruit salad.
Then read you a chapter from *Alice*,
rub your feet, feel you let go down the tunnel
of sleep, kiss the soft drapes of your cheek,
greedily receive a ghost of a smile, and leave.

Nil by Mouth

Still no swallow, so we'd brought things to smell:
lavender was in bloom and I'd plucked rosemary
trudging the dual carriageway from Silver Street.

Tessa brought various kinds of mint
from her Berkshire garden. You grunted
what we took to be approval. Encouraged,

I'd brought essential oils today. You had me repeat
their names: chamomile, geranium, frankincense,
rose. You nostrils quivered at each sniff.

Then from the twilit depths of your confusion,
as if the oils had cleared some mental passageways
like menthol for the mind, with just a whiff

of a smile, you announced your plan.
You can leave the bottles in the drawer,
and we can have some more tomorrow,

instead of listening to music. One is familiar
with the music, you know. But one isn't
familiar with this. It's very ... interesting.

Along the dual carriageway I walk on air,
become familiar with this ballooning
happiness, held on a rope of grief.

We Got the Hallstand

Bulky with anoraks,
clumps of woolly hats,
surrounded by recycling in sacks,

its elegance was never evident
on the lino in your hall,
but I was adamant.

Stripped of your outdoor apparel,
its dimensions were formidable,
but it *was* beautiful.

Almost art nouveau.
Honeyed oak.
Fluted and fretted and bowed.

I must have realised
we had nowhere to put it:
we'd just downsized.

For a year and a half, we edged
between the kitchen table
and the hallstand wedged

up against the window.
It blocked out light, gathered
dust on top, lists and keys below.

It cost twenty thousand pounds to build
the vestibule to put it in.
You'd left us nothing in your will.

I thought it would at least be useful:
a place for coats and shoes,
but when it stood in our new hall

I put an orchid in an antique jar,
one perfect pebble and, on the floor,
an oriental rug once used for prayer.

Your sole bequest became an empty space.
I wish I could have seen your face.

Slackening

Pouring your muesli helps assuage my guilt
while you get dressed to catch the twelve past eight
knowing I'll take my tea back to our quilt
still warm, to read. I stay pyjama-ed till quite late
these days. Last week's storms have stripped the trees.
It's winter. Easy to find excuses not to swim.
We don't need Google to tell us it will freeze
again tonight. Easier to sink another evening in.

So life winds down in loose, uneasy patterns.
We sort of rationalise our letting go of dreams.
Skin's surface, like stems of green things, slackens,
but affection does a better job than creams;
while the habit of acceptance makes failing
memories, eyesight, backs, plainish sailing.

Grand!

We cancelled classes, booked our flights
with days to spare, and now you're late.

We're ready. It's all in place. We know
the rules and route by rote. We wait.

Today the stars and stripes flap in rain.
We hover by our silent 'phones. You're late.

Your room is perfect, fresh and pink.
Your tiny clothes in neat rows wait

sweetly balled up tight in drawers,
tucked in with love, but now you're late.

They're doing all they can, they say,
you should be born by night. Right. We wait.

We yawn and stretch and watch the clock.
Another birthday passed. It's really late.

Your sleepsuits yawn, bibs long to scatter
milky stinky round the place – but wait!

For now the toe-sized socks begin to wriggle
the little caps raise themselves to see,
jump suits suppress the urge to bounce and giggle
and now the clock shows early hours, not late

at all, for here you are, tight folded, pink and shiny,
blue eyes wide open saying, *Just you wait!*

Seen in Sheffield

This is what boys are for! To strip
to the hip-sagging baggy pants;
shrug, slouch, then somersault to the brim
of the fountain; cat crawl the wall,
cartwheel, lazy-vault a stone plinth,
bend knees and flat foot it free-style,
frog-fashion, down all seven levels
of stone slabs sliced by blades of water.

This is what boys do: brace
on the handrail of city steps, spring
so that two feet lunge up to stand
on the next rail. Let go, drop back, land
squarely in size 12 trainers on the pavement.
Stroll back to the crowd, unflinching,
unsmiling, like no one's watching. Cool
as this cutting edge curve of water on steel.

This is what public sculpture's for: to mirror
these moves. This is what public spaces are for.
This is what this Saturday afternoon's for:
sliding down stone bannisters on one hip,
September not quite here. This
is what boys are: poems freed in air
above the sandwich wrappers in Sheaf Square
breakfalling among pigeons.

Focussing

A path tamped raw by many boots.
Hummocks of dead heather.
Rashes of ash-coloured stems
in petrified dance
where heath fires burned last summer.

Bilberry stalks erect as samphire.
Caramel tongues of beech leaves.
Frost pockets that would stay all day
hold a few spoonfuls of snow.

On the near horizon, tussocks
of dry grasses charged with light.

Sleek as a limestone horse,
a streak of snow leaps
to the crest above Eyam
with the telegraph mast.

And down there,
with the folds of Froggatt and Curbar
receding like islands in mist behind her,
Pauline, painting.

She's taken root by the stile in the wall
with her board and brushes
facing the sweep of Stanage

sees carmine bleeding
into plum and peat-black shadows ,
cadmium flaring from indigo,
a manganese sheen of sky.

Her hand swoops loosely
from the line of the horizon
discovering depths
dipping and surfacing
following the instinct of water.

Wet sketches scatter at her feet
like sea birds landing.

A Knowledge of Meadows

Site of Special Scientific Interest,
a sign had said, evoking fences,
closure, inspections. Not this
damp muddle where air is heavy
with the breath of meadowsweet,
unruly above betony, darts of orchid,
sparks of ragged robin,
hoary willow herb, bloody spears
of sorrel, rock roses: a holy hash
of Flora's things, half hidden
by high hazel already speckled
with pea green clusters,
the milk teeth of nuts.

That's a native small-leaved maple
and an airy space of aspens whispers
over a hollow at the bottom of the field.
I feel a marsh of past meadows
in me; shift through mist to bogs
of marigolds and lady's smock,
and rushes we'd peel all the way
to school, not knowing that before
schools began, their wicks
lit the lamps of history.

Now, framed in a gap in hawthorn,
lake bright, pale as bulbs:
a group of ponies, all the colours
of summer clouds. Their backs are bare
horizons, their bellies, globes.
Muzzles lift curiously, manes
raise question marks as they swerve
towards me, and noses nuzzle me,
hot with scientific interest.

A Local Habitation and a Name

We can see them all
over Blacka Moor, near Sheffield:
stonechat, linnet, sparrowhawk,
wheatear and woodcock.

> *though we may not know them*

In marshes near Redcar
wade gadwall and pochard.

> *nor who on earth named them*

On Redesdale
marlin and peregrine fly
and dippers dive.

> *though no one's watching*

They're still on the wing
near Kirkby Stephen:
the Northern Brown Argos
(whose egg is laid on the upper side
of the young leaf of the Rock Rose)
and the Green Fritillary
(whose caterpillar feeds on Dog Violet).

> *will their names outlive them?*

Somewhere near Weston, the orchids
– Green Winged, or Early Purple,
followed by Autumn Lady's Tresses –
are visited by the Grizzled Skipper
and Grayling.

> *or will they fly on,*
> *nameless, when we've gone?*

Unpainted Desert

We had our one blanket, and the colours in it
had names. Names of the plants from this land
in the times when the desert still flowered.
So we could name all the colours of grains of sand.

The yellows: rabbit brush, cliff rose and snakeweed.
Browns were onions, oak bark and tea.
Deep red was juniper, but most precious of all
was a pink from a shrub called purple bee.

These grains were so few, they were kept in a skull
of a grasshopper the wind had spun in. And we'd ask
and ask, what were rabbits, what were bees,
what was a snake, and what the colour of grass?

A brighter, cooler colour than we'd ever seen,
they'd said. The colour of wet, the colour of clean.

Wild Relatives

One rush hour on the Underground
that year, foetal elephants swam
all filmy pink on everyone's front page.
Our communal unconscious
held its breath. Trains floated
in unspoken tenderness.

I felt that sway again, under straddled
thighs, the shudder and steady
as the path tipped slippery to the river.
Alarm at a trunk raised trumpeting
wild relatives, gathered like shadows
among the baobabs, watching

the tame orphans we were riding.
Remembered, too, old eyes, dwarfed
by the crackled expanse of cranium,
hold mine, as the baby's trunk,
thicker than an arm, wetlipped
peanuts from my tingling palm.

Another day, a herd straddled
nonchalant around our open jeep,
not caring to change their route
at our incursion. A nudge would topple
us, but they flowed gravely by:
quiet river of elephantkind.

Ganesh now stands on our windowsill,
silver-etched with signs, sparkling
with elephant aura.
It was he who carried me,
when I journeyed shamanically,
ears tyrannosaurus butterflies.

Fourth Floor, Harvey Nichols:
a waste of silks and sushi. Handbags
of snakeskin, crocodile. Afternoon teas.
Mesmerised, we drift the aisles.
Discreet designer label on a grey hide
jacket reads – I put my glasses on – *elefant*.

Mammoth Memory

We slept standing, only our hooves could fend the ice.
We carried heat deep in our core in a forest of fur, frozen
at dawn, our snoring a rumble of thunder on the plains.

The old and the youngest hemmed in at the heart of the herd,
we cleaved the steppes, shovelling snow with our tusks,
grazing at the edges of ice sheets, pulping the crust
of the tundra – a maquis of bristles, dog lichen
and spikey sedge – in the churns of our bellies.

A musth was a rare thing. We were all heft and habit.
Even fear came slowly, like the erosion of cold.
Mostly, when the journeys were made, and memories
shared, an old one died standing, held up by the press
till she drew her last breath, only then lowered kindly,
lingered over and left.

We'd known lightning. It's flash. Even its singe.
But your arrows speed level. Burn straight into flesh.
Pierce through skin to jag bone, sever artery,
make spurt life-blood like geyser.

A lightning-quick death. We are all in musth now.
A tornado of terror: ruminating mass turned mayhem.
Pelts are rent, ribs cracked, tusks splintered.
We trample the carnage of ourselves.

Oversteps Books Ltd

The Oversteps list includes books by the following poets:

David Grubb, Giles Goodland, Alex Smith, Will Daunt, Patricia Bishop, Christopher Cook, Jan Farquarson, Charles Hadfield, Mandy Pannett, Doris Hulme, James Cole, Helen Kitson, Bill Headdon, Avril Bruton, Marianne Larsen, Anne Lewis-Smith, Mary Maher, Genista Lewes, Miriam Darlington, Anne Born, Glen Phillips, Rebecca Gethin, W H Petty, Melanie Penycate, Andrew Nightingale, Caroline Carver, John Stuart, Ann Segrave, Rose Cook, Jenny Hope, Christopher North, Hilary Elfick, Jennie Osborne, Anne Stewart, Oz Hardwick, Angela Stoner, Terry Gifford, Michael Swan, Denise Bennett, Maggie Butt, Anthony Watts, Joan McGavin, Robert Stein, Graham High, Ross Cogan, Ann Kelley, A C Clarke, Diane Tang, Susan Taylor, R V Bailey, Alwyn Marriage, John Daniel, Simon Williams, Kathleen Kummer, Jean Atkin, Charles Bennett, Elisabeth Rowe, Marie Marshall, Ken Head and Robert Cole.

For details of all these books, information about Oversteps and up-to-date news, please look at our website:

www.overstepsbooks.com